The A to Z Knock-Knock Joke Book

If you love knock-knock jokes,
and think nothing beats making people laugh,
then this book will knock you out!

The A to Z Knock-Knock Joke Book is a thumping
collection of over 300 jokes. The jokes are
ordered alphabetically, so you can chuckle your
way from A to Z, or search for a joke about
your favorite topic. From an amusing aardvark
to zany zinc, the laughs won't stop!

The A to Z Knock-Knock Joke Book will have your
friends and family banging on your door for more!

Knock, knock. Who's there?
AARDVARK. Aardvark who?
Aardvark a million miles for one of your smiles!

Knock, knock. Who's there?
ABEL. Abel who?
Abel to leap tall buildings in a single bound!

CHORTLE!

Knock, knock. Who's there?
ADAM. Adam who?
Adam up and tell me the total!

Knock, knock. Who's there?
ADORE. Adore who?
Adore is between you and me,
so please open up!

Knock, knock. Who's there?
ALADDIN. Aladdin who?
Aladdin a lady want a word with you!

Knock, knock. Who's there?
ALASKA. Alaska who?
Alaska to open the door again!

Knock, knock. Who's there?
ALBEE. Albee who?
Well, Albee a monkey's uncle!

Knock, knock. Who's there?
ALBERT. Albert who?
Albert you can't guess who this is!

Knock, knock. Who's there?
ALEC. Alec who?
Alec-tricity. Isn't that a shock?

Knock, knock. Who's there?
ALEX. Alex who?
Alex-plain when you open the door!

HAHAHA!

Knock, knock. Who's there?
ALFRED. Alfred who?
Alfred the needle if you sew!

Knock, knock. Who's there?
ALICE. Alice who?
Alice fair in love and war!

Knock, knock. Who's there?
ALLIGATOR. Alligator who?
Alligator for her birthday was a card!

Knock, knock. Who's there?
ALLISON. Allison who?
Allison to the radio every morning!

Knock, knock. Who's there?
ALPACA. Alpaca who?
Alpaca the suitcase, you load up the car!

BWAHAHA!

6

Knock, knock. Who's there?
ALVIN. Alvin who?
I'm Alvin a great time, how about you?

Knock, knock. Who's there?
AMIGO. Amigo who?
Amigo to bed now. I'm exhausted!

Knock, knock. Who's there?
AMOS. Amos who?
Amos-quito!

Knock, knock. Who's there?
AMY. Amy who?
Amy-fraid I've forgotten!

Knock, knock. Who's there?
ANDY. Andy who?
Andy bit me again! OUCH!

Knock, knock. Who's there?
ANITA. Anita who?
Anita drink of water, so please let me in!

Knock, knock. Who's there?
ANNA. Anna who?
Anna partridge in a pear tree!

Knock, knock. Who's there?
ANNE. Anne who?
Anne apple fell on my head!

Knock, knock. Who's there?
ANNIE. Annie who?
Annie thing you can do, I can do better!

Knock, knock. Who's there?
ARMENIA. Armenia who?
Armenia every word I say!

CACKLE!

Knock, knock. Who's there?
BABY OWL. Baby Owl who?
Baby owl see you later!

Knock, knock. Who's there?
BACON. Bacon who?
Bacon a cake for your birthday!

Knock, knock. Who's there?
BARBARA. Barbara who?
Barbara black sheep, have you any wool?

Knock, knock. Who's there?
BARBIE. Barbie who?
Barbie Q. Chicken!

HAHAHA!

Knock, knock. Who's there?
BARRY. Barry who?
Barry the treasure so no one will find it!

Knock, knock. Who's there?
BED. Bed who?
Bed you can't guess who it is!

Knock, knock. Who's there?
BEETS. Beets who?
Beets me!

Knock, knock. Who's there?
BELLA. Bella who?
Bella the ball!

Knock, knock. Who's there?
BEN. Ben who?
Ben away for a long time!

GIGGLE!

Knock, knock. Who's there?
BETTY. Betty who?
Betty-bye time, good night!

Knock, knock. Who's there?
BOLIVIA. Bolivia who?
I don't Bolivia had the pleasure!

Knock, knock. Who's there?
BOO. Boo who?
Oh, stop that crying!

Knock, knock. Who's there?
BROKEN PENCIL. Broken pencil who?
Oh, don't worry, it's pointless!

Knock, knock. Who's there?
BUTTER. Butter who?
Butter be quick, I have to go to the bathroom!

Knock, knock. Who's there?
BUTTON. Button who?
Button in is not polite!

HA HA!

Knock, knock. Who's there?
CAESAR. Caesar who?
Caesar quick, she's winning the race!

Knock, knock. Who's there?
CANDICE. Candice who?
Candice door open, or what?

Knock, knock. Who's there?
CANDY. Candy who?
Candy cow jump over the moon?

Knock, knock. Who's there?
CANNELLONI. Cannelloni who?
Cannelloni some money until next week?

HAH!

Knock, knock. Who's there?
CANOE. Canoe who?
Canoe come out and play?

Knock, knock. Who's there?
CARGO. Cargo who?
Cargo beep, beep and vroom, vroom!

Knock, knock. Who's there?
CARL. Carl who?
Carl go if you turn the key in the ignition!

Knock, knock. Who's there?
CARMEN. Carmen who?
Carmen get it!

Knock, knock. Who's there?
CASH. Cash who?
No thanks, but I'll have some peanuts!

Knock, knock. Who's there?
CEREAL. Cereal who?
Cereal pleasure to meet you!

Knock, knock. Who's there?
CHAD. Chad who?
Chad to make your acquaintance!

Knock, knock. Who's there?
CHAIR. Chair who?
Chair up, it's not so bad!

Knock, knock. Who's there?
CHERRY. Cherry who?
Cherry-oh! Goodbye!

Knock, knock. Who's there?
CHESTER. Chester who?
Chester minute, don't you recognize me?

Knock, knock. Who's there?
CINDY. Cindy who?
Cindy next one in, please!

Knock, knock. Who's there?
CLAIRE. Claire who?
Claire the way, I'm coming through!

Knock, knock. Who's there?
COLLEEN. Colleen who?
Colleen up this mess!

HAHAHA!

Knock, knock. Who's there?
CONRAD. Conrad who?
Conrad-ulations! That was a good knock-knock joke!

Knock, knock. Who's there?
COTTON. Cotton who?
Cotton a trap, can you get me out?

Knock, knock. Who's there?
COWS GO. Cows go who?
Cows go "moo," not who!

Knock, knock. Who's there?
DANIELLE. Danielle who?
Danielle at me, I heard you the first time!

Knock, knock. Who's there?
DAWN. Dawn who?
Dawn do anything I wouldn't do.

TEE-HEE!

Knock, knock. Who's there?
DENIAL. Denial who?
Denial is a river in Egypt!

Knock, knock. Who's there?
DESDEMONA. Desdemona who?
Desdemona Lisa have a smile on her face?

Knock, knock. Who's there?
DISHES. Dishes who?
Dishes the police!

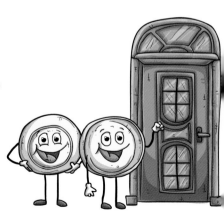

Knock, knock. Who's there?
DORIS. Doris who?
Doris locked, that's why I'm knocking!

Knock, knock. Who's there?
DOUBLE. Double who?
W!

Knock, knock. Who's there?
DOZEN. Dozen who?
Dozen anybody want to let me in?

Knock, knock. Who's there?
DRAGON. Dragon who?
Dragon you're feet to get to the door, aren't you?

Knock, knock. Who's there?
DWAYNE. Dwayne who?
Dwayne the bathtub! It's overflowing!

E

Knock, knock. Who's there?
EAMON. Eamon who?
Eamon a good mood today, can I come in?

Knock, knock. Who's there?
EAR. Ear who?
Ear you go!

Knock, knock. Who's there?
EARL. Earl who?
Earl be willing to tell you when you open this door!

Knock, knock. Who's there?
EGG. Egg who?
Egg-cited to see you!

BWAHAHA!

Knock, knock. Who's there?
ELLA. Ella who?
Ella-vator. Doesn't that give you a lift?

E

Knock, knock. Who's there?
ELLIE. Ellie who?
Ellie-phants are charging! Quick, let me in!

Knock, knock. Who's there?
ELSIE. Elsie who?
Elsie you around!

Knock, knock. Who's there?
ESTHER. Esther who?
Esther anything I can do for you?

Knock, knock. Who's there?
EVAN. Evan who?
Evan is a place on Earth!

Knock, knock. Who's there?
EYESORE. Eyesore who?
Eyesore do like you!

CACKLE!

Knock, knock. Who's there?
FALAFEL. Falafel who?
Falafel my bike and hurt my knee!

Knock, knock. Who's there?
FELIX. Felix who?
Felix my popsicle, I'll scream!

Knock, knock. Who's there?
FIGS. Figs who?
Figs the doorbell, it's broken!

Knock, knock. Who's there?
FLEAS. Fleas who?
Fleas a jolly good fellow!

Knock, knock. Who's there?
FLETCHER. Fletcher who?
Fletcher self go!

Knock, knock. Who's there?
FOUR EGGS. Four eggs who?
Four eggs-ample!

Knock, knock. Who's there?
FRANCIS. Francis who?
Francis a country in Europe!

Knock, knock. Who's there?
FRANK. Frank who?
Frank you for being my friend!

Knock, knock. Who's there?
FRED. Fred who?
Who's a Fred of the Big Bad Wolf?

GUFFAW!

Knock, knock. Who's there?
FREDDIE. Freddie who?
Freddie or not, here I come!

Knock, knock. Who's there?
GENOA. Genoa who?
Genoa good joke?

Knock, knock. Who's there?
GIDEON. Gideon who?
Gideon your horse and let's go!

CHORTLE!

Knock, knock. Who's there?
GLADYS. Gladys who?
Gladys Friday, aren't you?

Knock, knock. Who's there?
GOAT. Goat who?
Goat to the door and find out!

Knock, knock. Who's there?
GOOSE. Goose who?
Goose what I'm going to do if you don't open this door?

Knock, knock. Who's there?
GOPHER. Gopher who?
Gopher help! I'm stuck in the mud!

Knock, knock. Who's there?
GORILLA. Gorilla who?
Gorilla me a cheese sandwich, please!

Knock, knock. Who's there?
GRANT. Grant who?
Grant me a wish!

Knock, knock. Who's there?
GUS. Gus who?
That's what you're supposed to do!

Knock, knock. Who's there?
GWEN. Gwen who?
Gwen will I see you again?

Knock, knock. Who's there?
HAL. Hal who?
Hal-o, how are you doing?

Knock, knock. Who's there?
HALIBUT. Halibut who?
Halibut you open the door and let me in?

Knock, knock. Who's there?
HANDEL. Handel who?
Handel with care!

Knock, knock. Who's there?
HANK. Hank who?
Hank you!

Knock, knock. Who's there?
HANS. Hans who?
Hans off the table!

LOL!

Knock, knock. Who's there?
HARLOW. Harlow who?
Harlow can you go?

Knock, knock. Who's there?
HAROLD. Harold who?
Harold do you think I am?

Knock, knock. Who's there?
HARRIET. Harriet who?
Harriet all my lunch, so I'm hungry!

Knock, knock. Who's there?
HARRY. Harry who?
Harry up, it's cold out here!

Knock, knock. Who's there?
HATCH. Hatch who?
Bless you!

HAW-HAW!

Knock, knock. Who's there?
HAWAII. Hawaii who?
I'm fine, thanks. Hawaii you?

Knock, knock. Who's there?
HEIDI. Heidi who?
Heidi-cided to come over to play!

Knock, knock. Who's there?
HERRING. Herring who?
I'm herring some good jokes today!

Knock, knock. Who's there?
HONEYBEE. Honeybee who?
Honeybee a dear and open this door!

Knock, knock. Who's there?
HONEYCOMB. Honeycomb who?
Honeycomb your hair, it's a mess!

Knock, knock. Who's there?
HOO. Hoo who?
You talk like an owl!

Knock, knock. Who's there?
HOWARD. Howard who?
Howard I know?

SNICKER!

Knock, knock. Who's there?
HOWL. Howl who?
Howl you find out unless you open the door?

Knock, knock. Who's there?
HUGH. Hugh who?
Hugh have got to be kidding!

Knock, knock. Who's there?
HUGO. Hugo who?
Hugo your way, I'll go mine!

Knock, knock. Who's there?
ICE CREAM. Ice cream who?
Ice cream if you don't let me in!

Knock, knock. Who's there?
ICE CREAM SODA. Ice cream soda who?
Ice cream soda whole world will hear me!

Knock, knock. Who's there?
ICING. Icing who?
Icing so loud, all the neighbors complain!

Knock, knock. Who's there?
ICY. Icy who?
Icy you inside, can I come in?

Knock, knock. Who's there?
IDA. Ida who?
Ida like to be your friend!

CACKLE!

Knock, knock. Who's there?
IGUANA. Iguana who?
Iguana hold your hand!

Knock, knock. Who's there?
IKE. Ike who?
Ike-n't stop laughing!

Knock, knock. Who's there?
IMMA. Imma who?
Imma getting cold! Open the door!

Knock, knock. Who's there?
IMOGEN. Imogen who?
Imogen life without chocolate!

Knock, knock. Who's there?
IONA. Iona who?
Iona new car!

HAHAHA!

Knock, knock. Who's there?
IRELAND. Ireland who?
Ireland you some money, but you must pay it back!

Knock, knock. Who's there?
IRENE. Irene who?
Irene and Irene, but you don't answer the door!

Knock, knock. Who's there?
IRIS. Iris who?
Iris you were here!

Knock, knock. Who's there?
IRISH. Irish who?
Irish I knew some better knock-knock jokes!

Knock, knock. Who's there?
ISABEL. Isabel who?
Isabel working? I had to knock!

BWAHAHA!

Knock, knock. Who's there?
ISABELLA. Isabella who?
Isabella on a bike a good idea?

Knock, knock. Who's there?
ISLE OF. Isle of who?
Isle of you, too!

Knock, knock. Who's there?
ISSAC. Issac who?
Issac of these knock-knock jokes!

Knock, knock. Who's there?
IVAN. Ivan who?
Ivan to be alone!

Knock, knock. Who's there?
IVOR. Ivor who?
Ivor good mind not to tell you now!

TEE-HEE!

Knock, knock. Who's there?
JAMAICA. Jamaica who?
Jamaica mistake?

Knock, knock. Who's there?
JAWS. Jaws who?
Jaws truly!

Knock, knock. Who's there?
JESS. Jess who?
Jess me and my shadow!

Knock, knock. Who's there?
JESTER. Jester who?
Jester minute. I'm still thinking!

Knock, knock. Who's there?
JOAN. Joan who?
Joan you remember me?

J

Knock, knock. Who's there?
JOE. Joe who?
Joe away, I'm not talking to you!

Knock, knock. Who's there?
JUICY. Juicy who?
Juicy any good movies lately?

LOL!

Knock, knock. Who's there?
JUNE. June who?
June know how long I've been knocking out here?

Knock, knock. Who's there?
JUSTICE. Justice who?
Justice as I thought, you don't remember me!

Knock, knock. Who's there?
JUSTIN. Justin who?
Justin the neighborhood and thought
I'd come over!

Knock, knock. Who's there?
KAY. Kay who?
Kay, L, M, N, O, P, Q, R, S, T, U, V, W, X, Y, Z!

Knock, knock. Who's there?
KEANU. Keanu who?
Keanu let me in? It's cold out here.

Knock, knock. Who's there?
KENT. Kent who?
Kent you tell who it is?

Knock, knock. Who's there?
KENYA. Kenya who?
Kenya open the door, please?

Knock, knock. Who's there?
KERMIT. Kermit who?
Kermit a crime and you'll get caught!

GIGGLE!

Knock, knock. Who's there?
LARVA. Larva who?
I'd larva cup of tea, thank you!

Knock, knock. Who's there?
LASS. Lass who?
That's what a cowboy uses, isn't it?

Knock, knock. Who's there?
LEAF. Leaf who?
Leaf me alone!

Knock, knock. Who's there?
LENA. Lena who?
Lena little closer and I'll tell you!

Knock, knock. Who's there?
LES. Les who?
Les go for a swim!

Knock, knock. Who's there?
LETTUCE. Lettuce who?
Lettuce in, it's cold out here!

CHUCKLE!

Knock, knock. Who's there?
LINDA. Linda who?
Linda hand, I can't be expected to do it all by myself!

Knock, knock. Who's there?
LIONEL. Lionel who?
Lionel roar if you don't feed him!

Knock, knock. Who's there?
LITTLE OLD LADY. Little old lady who?
Wow, I didn't know you could yodel!

Knock, knock. Who's there?
LUKE. Luke who?
Luke through the window and see!

Knock, knock. Who's there?
MABEL. Mabel who?
Mabel doesn't work either!

Knock, knock. Who's there?
MAE. Mae who?
Mae I please come in?

HE HE!

Knock, knock. Who's there?
MAGGOT. Maggot who?
Maggot these new jeans today,
do you like them?

Knock, knock. Who's there?
MAJOR! Major who?
Major get up and answer the door!

Knock, knock. Who's there?
MANDY. Mandy who?
Mandy lifeboats, we're sinking!

Knock, knock. Who's there?
MANGO. Mango who?
Mango to the door and open it!

Knock, knock. Who's there?
MATH. Math who?
Math potatoes are my favorite!

Knock, knock. Who's there?
MATTHEW. Matthew who?
Matthew lace has come undone, will you tie it?

Knock, knock. Who's there?
MAX. Max who?
Max no difference!

SNICKER!

Knock, knock. Who's there?
MIKEY. Mikey who?
Mikey doesn't fit in the keyhole!

Knock, knock. Who's there?
MONEY. Money who?
Money hurts when I run.

Knock, knock. Who's there?
MOOSE. Moose who?
Moose you be so nosy?

Knock, knock. Who's there?
MUFFIN. Muffin who?
Muffin the matter with me,
how about you?

Knock, knock. Who's there?
MUSTACHE. Mustache who?
Mustache you a question, but I'll
shave it for later!

Knock, knock. Who's there?
MYTH. Myth who?
I myth you, too!

Knock, knock. Who's there?
NANA. Nana who?
Nana your business!

Knock, knock. Who's there?
NEEDLE. Needle who?
Needle little help getting through this door!

Knock, knock. Who's there?
NICHOLAS. Nicholas who?
Nicholas half as much as a dime!

Knock, knock. Who's there?
NOAH. Noah who?
Noah good place I can get something to eat?

HA HA!

Knock, knock. Who's there?
NOBEL. Nobel who?
Nobel, so I kept knocking!

Knock, knock. Who's there?
NOISE. Noise who?
Noise to see you!

Knock, knock. Who's there?
NORMA. Norma who?
Norma-lly I have my key!

HAW-HAW!

Knock, knock. Who's there?
NORWAY. Norway who?
Norway will I leave until you open this door!

Knock, knock. Who's there?
NOSE. Nose who?
I nose plenty more knock-knock jokes!

Knock, knock. Who's there?
NUISANCE. Nuisance who?
What's nuisance yesterday?

Knock, knock. Who's there?
OLGA. Olga who?
Olga way when I'm good and ready!

Knock, knock. Who's there?
OLIVE. Olive who?
Olive across the road!

Knock, knock. Who's there?
OLIVER. Oliver who?
Oliver the world, people laugh at this joke!

Knock, knock. Who's there?
OLIVIA. Olivia who?
Olivia me alone!

Knock, knock. Who's there?
OMAR. Omar who?
Omar goodness! I'm locked out!

HAHAHA!

Knock, knock. Who's there?
ORANGE JUICE. Orange juice who?
Orange juice going to open this door?

Knock, knock. Who's there?
OSCAR. Oscar who?
Oscar silly question, get a silly answer!

Knock, knock. Who's there?
OTTO. Otto who?
I Otto know, but I can't remember!

Knock, knock. Who's there?
OWL. Owl who?
Owl aboard!

HAH!

Knock, knock. Who's there?
OZZIE. Ozzie who?
Ozzie you later!

Knock, knock. Who's there?
PASTA. Pasta who?
Pasta salt, please!

Knock, knock. Who's there?
PAT. Pat who?
Pat yourself on the back!

Knock, knock. Who's there?
PAUL. Paul who?
Paul up a chair and I'll tell you!

Knock, knock. Who's there?
PECAN. Pecan who?
Pecan on somebody your own size!

Knock, knock. Who's there?
PHILIP. Philip who?
Philip my glass, please. I'm so thirsty!

HAW-HAW!

44

Knock, knock. Who's there?
PHYLLIS. Phyllis who?
Phyllis in on the news!

Knock, knock. Who's there?
PIZZA. Pizza who?
Pizza real nice guy!

Knock, knock. Who's there?
POLICE. Police who?
Police stop telling these awful knock-knock jokes!

Knock, knock. Who's there?
POODLE. Poodle who?
Poodle little mustard on my hot dog, please!

SNICKER!

Knock, knock. Who's there?
PUDDING. Pudding who?
Pudding your shoes on before your pants is a silly idea!

Knock, knock. Who's there?
QUACK. Quack who?
Quack another bad joke and I'm leaving!

Knock, knock. Who's there?
QUEEN. Queen who?
Just had a shower and I'm queen as a whistle!

CHUCKLE!

Knock, knock. Who's there?
QUICHE. Quiche who?
Can I have a hug and a quiche?

Knock, knock. Who's there?
QUIET TINA. Quiet Tina who?
Quiet Tina library!

Knock, knock. Who's there?
QUINCY. Quincy who?
Quincy you through the window!

Knock, knock. Who's there?
RABBIT. Rabbit who?
Rabbit up carefully, it's fragile!

Knock, knock. Who's there?
RADIO. Radio who?
Radio not, here I come!

HE HE!

Knock, knock. Who's there?
RAY. Ray who?
Ray-member me?

Knock, knock. Who's there?
RHINO. Rhino who?
Rhino every joke there is!

Knock, knock. Who's there?
RHODA. Rhoda who?
Row, row, Rhoda boat!

Knock, knock. Who's there?
RITA. Rita who?
Rita book and you might learn something!

Knock, knock. Who's there?
ROLAND. Roland who?
A Roland stone gathers no moss!

SNICKER!

Knock, knock. Who's there?
ROME. Rome who?
Rome is where the heart is!

Knock, knock. Who's there?
ROWAN. Rowan who?
Rowan a boat is hard work!

Knock, knock. Who's there?
RUSSELL. Russell who?
Russell up something to eat, I'm starving!

S

Knock, knock. Who's there?
SABRINA. Sabrina who?
Sabrina long time since I last saw you!

Knock, knock. Who's there?
SACHA. Sacha who?
Sacha lot of questions!

Knock, knock. Who's there?
SADIE. Sadie who?
Sadie magic word and watch me disappear!

Knock, knock. Who's there?
SAFARI. Safari who?
Safari so good!

Knock, knock. Who's there?
SAM. Sam who?
Sam-day my prince will come!

S

Knock, knock. Who's there?
SANDY. Sandy who?
Sandy door, I just got a splinter!

Knock, knock. Who's there?
SARAH. Sarah who?
Sarah phone I can use?

HA HA!

Knock, knock. Who's there?
SCOLD. Scold who?
Scold enough out here to go ice-skating!

Knock, knock. Who's there?
SEA. Sea who?
Open the door and sea for yourself!

Knock, knock. Who's there?
SEYMOUR. Seymour who?
You'll Seymour if you look out of the window!

Knock, knock. Who's there?
SHELBY. Shelby who?
Shelby coming round the mountain when she comes!

Knock, knock. Who's there?
SHERWOOD. Sherwood who?
Sherwood like this door opened!

Knock, knock. Who's there?
SHIRLEY. Shirley who?
Shirley you must know me by now!

Knock, knock. Who's there?
SLOTH. Sloth who?
I sloth my phone or I'd have called!

Knock, knock. Who's there?
SNOW. Snow who?
Snow use, I forgot my name again!

S

Knock, knock. Who's there?
SPAIN. Spain who?
Spain to have to keep knocking on this door!

Knock, knock. Who's there?
SPELL. Spell who?
W. H. O.

Knock, knock. Who's there?
SPIDER. Spider who?
Spider what people say, I still like you!

Knock, knock. Who's there?
STOPWATCH. Stopwatch who?
Stopwatch you're doing and let me in!

CHORTLE!

Knock, knock. Who's there?
SUSAN. Susan who?
Susan socks keep your feet warm!

Knock, knock. Who's there?
TAD. Tad who?
Tad's all folks!

Knock, knock. Who's there?
TAMARA. Tamara who?
Tamara is Tuesday, today is Monday!

HAHAHA!

Knock, knock. Who's there?
TANK. Tank who?
You're welcome!

Knock, knock. Who's there?
TENNESSEE. Tennessee who?
Tennessee you tonight, please?

Knock, knock. Who's there?
TENNIS. Tennis who?
Tennis five plus five!

Knock, knock. Who's there?
TERESA. Teresa who?
Teresa green!

Knock, knock. Who's there?
THEODORE. Theodore who?
Theodore is stuck and won't open!

Knock, knock. Who's there?
TIBET. Tibet who?
Early Tibet, early to rise!

Knock, knock. Who's there?
TILLY. Tilly who?
Tilly comes I'm going to wait here!

Knock, knock. Who's there?
TINKERBELL. Tinkerbell who?
Tinkerbell is broken, so I'm knocking on her door!

CACKLE!

Knock, knock. Who's there?
TOBY. Toby who?
Toby or not to be, that is the question!

Knock, knock. Who's there?
TOOTH. Tooth who?
Tooth or dare?

Knock, knock. Who's there?
TORI. Tori who?
Tori I bumped into you!

Knock, knock. Who's there?
TROY. Troy who?
Troy the bell if the knocking doesn't get anyone's attention!

Knock, knock. Who's there?
TURNIP. Turnip who?
Turnip the radio, I love this song!

Knock, knock. Who's there?
UDDER. Udder who?
Udder madness to leave me out here!

Knock, knock. Who's there??
UNA. Una who?
No, I don't—tell me!

Knock, knock. Who's there?
UNIT. Unit who?
Unit socks, I knit sweaters!

Knock, knock. Who's there?
UPHILL. Uphill who?
Uphill will take your headache away!

HAH!

Knock, knock. Who's there?
UTAH. Utah who?
Utah one who told me to knock!

Knock, knock. Who's there?
VALUE. Value who?
Value please open the door?

Knock, knock. Who's there?
VAMPIRE. Vampire who?
The vampire state building!

GUFFAW!

Knock, knock. Who's there?
VEAL CHOP. Veal chop who?
Veal chop around and see what
bargains we can pick up!

Knock, knock. Who's there?
VENICE. Venice who?
Venice your friend coming over?

Knock, knock. Who's there?
VERA. Vera who?
Vera all the good knock-knock jokes?

Knock, knock. Who's there?
VINCENT. Vincent who?
Vincent me here!

Knock, knock. Who's there?
VIOLA. Viola who?
Viola sudden you don't know me?

Knock, knock. Who's there?
VIOLET. Violet who?
Violet the cat out of the bag!

Knock, knock. Who's there?
VIPER. Viper who?
Viper nose, it's running!

Knock, knock. Who's there?
VOODOO. Voodoo who?
Voodoo you think you are talking to?

Knock, knock. Who's there?
WAFER. Wafer who?
I was wafer a long time, but now I'm back!

Knock, knock. Who's there?
WAITER. Waiter who?
Waiter minute while I tie my shoelaces!

Knock, knock. Who's there?
WATER. Water who?
Water way to answer the door!

Knock, knock. Who's there?
WATSON. Watson who?
Watson TV tonight?

CACKLE!

Knock, knock. Who's there?
WAYNE. Wayne who?
Wayne are you coming over to my house?

Knock, knock. Who's there?
WENDY. Wendy who?
Wendy wind blows, the cradle will rock!

Knock, knock. Who's there?
WHALE. Whale who?
Whale you be my best friend?

Knock, knock. Who's there?
WILMA. Wilma who?
Wilma snoring keep you awake all night?

Knock, knock. Who's there?
WIRE. Wire who?
Wire you asking? You know who I am!

Knock, knock. Who's there?
WOODEN SHOE. Wooden shoe who?
Wooden shoe like to hear another joke?

CHUCKLE!

Knock, knock. Who's there?
X. X who?
X-tremely pleased to meet you!

Knock, knock. Who's there?
XAVIER. Xavier who?
Xavier your breath and open the door!

Knock, knock. Who's there?
YACHTS UP. Yachts up who?
Yachts up, doc?

Knock, knock. Who's there?
YAH. Yah who?
I didn't know you were a cowboy!

Knock, knock. Who's there?
YETI. Yeti who?
Yeti-nother knock-knock joke!

Knock, knock. Who's there?
YORK. York who?
York coming over to my place for dinner?

Knock, knock. Who's there?
YORKIES. Yorkies who?
Yorkies don't unlock the door!

SNICKER!

Knock, knock. Who's there?
YUGO. Yugo who?
Yugo first, I'll be right behind you!

Knock, knock. Who's there?
YUKON. Yukon who?
Yukon say that again!

Knock, knock. Who's there?
YVONNE. Yvonne who?
Yvonne to be alone!

Z

Knock, knock. Who's there?
ZACH. Zach who?
Zach's all, folks!

Knock, knock. Who's there?
ZANY. Zany who?
Zany one home?

Knock, knock. Who's there?
ZEROES. Zeroes who?
Zeroes as fast as she can, but the boat doesn't move!

Knock, knock. Who's there?
ZESTING. Zesting who?
Zesting from zat bee still hurts!

Knock, knock. Who's there?
ZINC. Zinc who?
Do you zinc you can open the door?

GUFFAW!

LOL!

BWAHAHA!

HE HE!

CACKLE!

HA HA!

First American Edition 2021
Kane Miller, A Division of EDC Publishing
Copyright © Green Android Ltd 2020
Illustrated by Vasco Icuza

For information contact:
Kane Miller, A Division of EDC Publishing
P.O. Box 470663
Tulsa, OK 74147-0663
www.kanemiller.com
www.edcpub.com
www.usbornebooksandmore.com

Library of Congress Control Number: 2020936362

Printed and bound in Malaysia, January 2021
ISBN: 978-1-68464-210-6

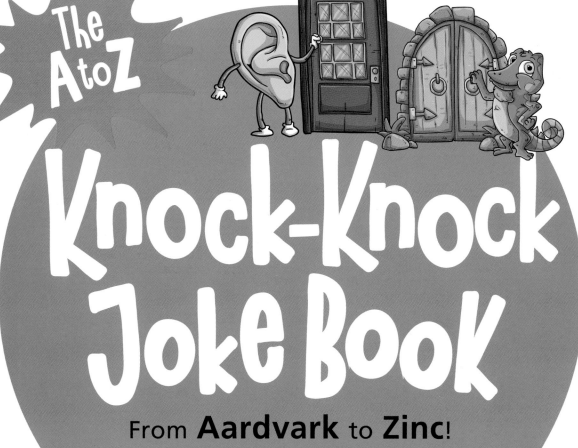

The A to Z

Knock-Knock Joke Book

From **Aardvark** to **Zinc**!

Illustrated by Vasco Icuza

Kane Miller
A DIVISION OF EDC PUBLISHING

HE HE!
LOL!
HAHAHA!
HA HA!
HAH!
TEE-HEE!
CACKLE!
CHORTLE!
GIGGLE!
BWAHAHA!